# Bookkeeping
## *The Ultimate Guide to Bookkeeping for Small Business*

# Contents

# Introduction

Whether you are just starting your business or have had your business for years, it is important to know bookkeeping.

Bookkeeping has been around for centuries. However, it has evolved over time to better help your business keep track of your finances.

Bookkeeping covers a long list of aspects that help the business owner make decisions about the company. To better understand bookkeeping, my goal is to help you get a good feel for knowing how to read the financial reports, the basics of bookkeeping, employees, understanding the balance sheet and income statement, and so much more.

Come along with me as we explore the world of bookkeeping and help you, the business owner, understand how to make sense out of bookkeeping.

As an added bonus, I have included a section for your business taxes. I also included a step-by-step process of preparing W-2 forms and the information that is needed for those. You will soon find out that there is more to it than just providing the information and typing it up on the W-2 form.

Keep reading and you will see what it takes to get on the same page as your bookkeeper. I always said, "It is not the business owner that runs the business. It is the business owner teamed up with the bookkeeper that truly runs the business."

Running a business can be fun and rewarding. However, if you do not have the basic knowledge of the fundamental financial skills needed, it can prove to be stressful as well.

Throughout this book you will learn the basics of bookkeeping and finding the right bookkeeper for you. As you go through it, you will also learn about the ledgers and journals. It is important that you know where your money is at all times. I also take the time to talk to you about hiring employees. Let's face it, if your business is going to grow above a certain level, you will eventually need to hire someone to work with you.

There is also a lot of software available to help you with all your bookkeeping needs, although not all accounting software is right for your business. We will take a look at a few of the top rated applications and give you both the good and bad of each one.

Don't forget, you also need to understand those scary financial statements. That's why we will take a look at the four main financial statements and break them down for you so that you can easily read and understand each one.

It does not matter if you have been in business for a couple of years or are just starting, you will be filing taxes at the end of the year. This is a lot of work and your bookkeeper can help you get prepared. Within the bonus chapter, I included a checklist for small businesses to help you along the way in knowing which documents you need to find and hold on to.

Did you know that as a business owner you can deduct a lot of your expenses? I included that as well. It is only a small list, and with a little research you could probably find more.

Finally, I also included, in detail, how to go about preparing, distributing, and filing the employees' W-2's.

So come along with me as we take this glorious adventure into bookkeeping for small businesses and give you the power to understand your businesses financial health.

# Chapter 1 – Bookkeeping Basics

Before we get started on breaking down bookkeeping, we need to look at some of the basics. I want you to have the ability to read your financial records and understand them. This will allow for you to know the financial aspect of your business. In turn, it will allow you to make good decisions that can increase the growth of your business.

## Double-Entry Method

Bookkeeping uses a method called the "Double-Entry Bookkeeping." This means that for every entry there is at least one debit and one credit.

I want you to remember this equation:

- Assets = Liabilities + Equity

This is the basic formula for the Double-Entry Method and will come into play with every transaction you make.

## Source Documents

Every transaction made will have a source document. Source documents could be anything from a contract to a gas receipt. If you spent the business's money then you will need some form of proof of how much you spent. These are the source documents.

These documents will give us all the information you will need to record it in the books. This includes referencing the source documents. Some software will allow you to attach the scanned file to the transaction so that at any time you can bring up the source document.

## End-Of-Period Procedures

End-of-Period Procedures relate to not only quarters. Even though all the transactions have been recorded throughout the months or year, they still are not read for preparing the financial reports.

To ensure that you have your books accurate for preparing the financial reports, you need to consider that there are procedures that need to happen at least at month-end, year-end, and the end of payroll year.

The following outline on the next page will show, as a guideline, what should be done during each time.

1. Month-End Procedures

   o Run the Company/Business Data Auditor

   o Reconcile your Bank Accounts

   o Review Reports

   o Send Customer Statements

   o Record Depreciation

   o Pay Payroll Taxes

   o Lock Periods

2. Year-End Procedures (to prepare for the new fiscal year)

   o Complete Month-End Tasks

   o Perform an Inventory Count

   o Provide Information to your Accountant

   o Enter End-of-Year Adjustments

   o Back Up your Company/Business File

   o Start New Fiscal Year

   o Optimize and Verify your Company/Business File

3. End of Payroll Year (to prepare for new fiscal year) - *NOTE: Do Not Update Tax Tables*

   o Run Your Last Payroll

- o Optimize and Verify your Company/Business File

- o Back Up your Company/Business File

- o Start a New Payroll Year

- o Install Product Updates

- o Run Your First Payroll

- o Restore Your Backup

- o Print Year-End Payroll Forms

- o Print Vendor 1099 Statements

- o Print Payroll Reports

# Compile the Adjusted Trial Balance

Making these adjustments are very important. When looking at which adjustments need to be made first, you need to gather and compile a spreadsheet that will allow for your trial balance entries as well as the adjustments.

Keep in mind that these adjustments are for correcting errors in the initial trial balance so that everything will come to balance. This form for the adjustments is an internal form but will be used for helping compile the financial statements. Now that automated systems like Xero and QuickBooks are used, the trial balance worksheet is not often practiced. However, it is still a good source document. This is in part due to the automated systems creating the reports for you.

The following is an example of what the worksheet may look like:

Frank's Financials

Trial Balance

August 31, 20XX

| | Unadjusted Trial Balance | Adjusted Entries | Adjusted Trial Balance |
|---|---|---|---|
| Cash | $60,000 | | $60,000 |
| Accounts Receivable | $180,000 | $50,000 | $230,000 |
| Inventory | $300,000 | | $300,000 |
| Fixed Assets (net) | $210,000 | | $210,000 |
| Accounts Payable | ($90,000) | | ($90,000) |
| Accrued Liabilities | ($50,000) | ($25,000) | ($75,000) |
| Notes Payable | ($420,000) | | ($420,000) |
| Equity | ($350,000) | | ($350,000) |
| Revenue | ($400,000) | ($50,000) | ($450,000) |
| Cost of Goods Sold | $290,000 | | $290,000 |
| Salaries | $200,000 | $25,000 | $225,000 |
| Payroll Taxes | $20,000 | | $20,000 |
| Rent | $35,000 | | $35,000 |

| | | | |
|---|---|---|---|
| Other Expenses | $15,000 | | $15,000 |
| Totals | $0.00 | $0.00 | $0.00 |

# Closing the Books

When closing your books at the end of a fiscal year, there are 4 areas that will need to be closed. These areas are temporary accounts and should be zeroed out at the end of each fiscal year.

First, create an Income Summary account. This is considered a holding area.

### Closing the Revenue Accounts

The first area that needs to be addressed are the revenue accounts. You will either Debit or Credit this account to close it out and have a zero balance. Then you will either Debit or Credit the Income Summary account to add that balance to the account. Remember if you Debit or Credit one account you must do the opposite for the other account to keep the books balanced.

### Closing the Expense Accounts

The second set of accounts are the expense accounts. You will do the same with these accounts as you did with the Revenue accounts. You must close out all expense accounts.

### Balancing the Income Summary

By name you should have an increase in the income summary for the revenue and a decrease for each of the expenses. Keep in mind that if the expenses are more than the revenue then it will be a negative number and considered a loss. However, if the revenue is more than the expenses then it is a gain or profit for that year.

### Closing the Income Summary

The last step in closing the book is to Debit or Credit the income summary account and do the same to the Retained Earnings Account, leaving a zero balance in the income summary account.

## Preparing Reports

A pretty important step is to prepare the reports or financial statements. Although there are so many reports that can be created, we are going to focus on the main reports as they are what is needed for a small business.

As a bookkeeper, you will need to get very familiar with the following reports:

- The Balance Sheet

- Income Statement

- Statement of Retained Earnings

- Statement of Cash Flow

Later in this book we will look more closely at each one of these statements and how to read them so that you can make sense out of your businesses financial standings.

# Chapter 2 – What's New in Bookkeeping for Small Business?

Bookkeeping is always changing and new software is always coming out. Let's look at some of these techniques and software programs that are out there for you to use as a small business owner.

## Open a Business Bank Account

You want to see your business succeed. However, how do you keep your personal finances separate from your business finances? The answer is simple; just open a business bank account.

It is extremely hard to see how your business is doing if you combine your business revenue and expenses with your personal. The best way is to check with your bank first to see if they have a business account available.

Using a spreadsheet is basic. Although, what if your business has inventory, employees, vendors, etc.? This is when an accounting or bookkeeping software could come in handy. My recommendation is QuickBooks or Xero as they both provide for these types of accounts.

## Choose the Best Bookkeeping Software for your Business

Choosing a software can vary based on your needs. At minimum, you will need a ledger or cashbook. The cashbook that would include the general journal and the ledges can easily be done using a spreadsheet like Microsoft Excel or Google Sheets. Remember, Google Sheet will allow you to save it through Google and have access to the file anywhere you are.

QuickBooks and Xero may not be the best for your business. Sometimes, the most difficult part is finding the software that works the best for your needs.

Let's look at a few different bookkeeping applications that may get you started. I will include QuickBooks and Xero.

**Intuit QuickBooks Online**

QuickBooks Online is by far the best accounting and bookkeeping software for small businesses. I like that you can link it to your bank account. This makes it easy to use and track money when linked to your business account. It makes it easy to reconcile the business account and the books. Although there is so much more to QuickBooks Online.

Just a few of the features within QuickBooks Online include:

- Invoicing

- Expense Tracking

- Inventory Management

- Purchase Ordering

- Reporting

As your business grows, you can upgrade your account between the top three tiers. This will allow you to have everything you need for your small business. Another part that is great about QuickBooks Online is that there are apps for your phone both through Android and iOS devices. The software is also compatible with most third-party applications.

QuickBooks Online also offers some of the best pricing. There are four tiers of pricing, depending on what you need for your business. It also offers a 30-day free trial. However, if you want to just jump right into it and go for the paid versions you will get a 50% discount for the first six months. That means if you are just starting your business you will have six months to make a little extra profit and get established before you need to pay full price.

The most basic is the Self-Employed plan. This plan is $10 per month. It is designed for independent contractors and freelancers. It allows the following:

- Track Mileage

- Track Income and Expenses

- Create Invoices

- Accept Payments

- Run Reports

Keep in mind the Self-Employed plan cannot be upgraded to a higher tier. It will require you to create and set up a new account.

The next tier is the Simple Start plan. With this plan, a single user is supported and costs $15 per month. This plan includes the following:

- Track Mileage

- Track Income and Expenses

- Create Invoices

- Accept Payments

- Run Reports

- Send Estimates

- Track Sales and Sales Tax

The next tier is the Essentials plan. This plan supports multiple users and costs $35 per month. This plan includes:

- Track Mileage

- Track Income and Expenses

- Create Invoices

- Accept Payments

- Run Reports

- Send Estimates

- Track Sales and Sales Tax

- Bill Management

- Time Tracking

The last tier is the Plus plan. This plan also allows for multiple users and costs $50 per month. This plan includes:

- Track Mileage

- Track Income and Expenses

- Create Invoices

- Accept Payments

- Run Reports

- Send Estimates

- Track Sales and Sales Tax

- Bill Management

- Time Tracking

- Track Inventory

- Create Budgets

- Pay Independent Contractors that use the 1099 form

Like most small business, you will eventually have employees that you will need to pay. With QuickBooks Online, you can add this feature to any of the top three tiers for an additional monthly cost.

The best part is QuickBooks Online is very user friendly and easy to use. This software also has a good timesaving feature that you need in any good accounting and bookkeeping program. It will keep track of due dates for invoices, sync your business bank account, track your credit card transactions, and so much more. This allows you to focus more time on the business and less time on the books while maintaining accurate bookkeeping throughout your business and giving you a great outlook of the financials of the business. Another good timesaving feature that puts QuickBooks Online on top is that you can send out invoices to customers, allowing them to pay online at a click of a button.

Like with any application, things tend to go wrong with the program itself. That is why QuickBooks Online offers both phone and chat support. You can access this from the company website making it easier and quicker to get issues resolved and have you up and running again without missing a sale.

QuickBooks Online is account approved. This means that no matter what your needs are you can give your accountant access to your books. Remember, that your account will not take up a spot in your users that you give access to.

Like all programs there are some limitations, although with QuickBooks Online it seems like the sky is the limit. The limitations really lay within the mobile apps. Here are the things you can do with the mobile apps:

- Send Invoices

- Reconcile Transactions

- Take photos of receipts and attach to expenses

- View customer information and add new customers

- View dashboard data, such as account balance, profit and loss reports, and open and past due invoices.

After looking through what the app can do, if you feel like that works perfect then QuickBooks Online is the perfect software for you. However, if you prefer doing most of your accounting and bookkeeping through your phone, then there is another accounting and bookkeeping software choice for you.

**Xero**

If you would rather use a PC or a Mac, Xero has a lot to offer. Xero is by far the best accounting and bookkeeping software for Mac users. It easy to use and learn. What I like about Xero are the videos. Everything you do in Xero will have a video that will help you learn the software.

Xero also has comparable prices and is listed into three different plans. The starter plan is $9 per month. It does have some limitations. The features of the starter plan are:

- Unlimited Users

- Limit to Five Invoices per month

- Limit to Five Bills per month

- Limit to 20 Transaction Reconciliations per month

The standard plan is $30 per month. This includes:

- Unlimited Users

- Unlimited Invoices

- Unlimited Bills

- Unlimited Transaction Reconciliations

- Payroll for up to Five Employees

The premium plan is $70 per month. Which includes:

- Unlimited Users

- Unlimited Invoices

- Unlimited Bills

- Unlimited Transaction Reconciliations

- Payroll for up to 10 Employees. *Note: this can be adjusted to support more employees if needed.*

- Supports Multiple Currencies. *Note: this is a great feature if you do international business.*

The best part is that there are not any long-term contracts for using Xero. That means you can change at any time without having additional fees. There is also a free 30-day trial to let you try and find out if it will be the best for your business.

Much like QuickBooks Online, Xero also has many timesaving features. You can send out invoices electronically, which also allows for your customers to pay online easily. You can also turn quotes and estimates into invoices with only a few clicks. This allows for you to give a customer a quote and if they agree to go with your services you can turn that quote into an invoice and get paid.

With your business bank account linked to Xero, the system will allow you to set scheduled payments and manually pay the bills. This helps save time and ensures that all bills are paid on time and you do not need to worry about past-dues and late fees.

If you need to claim an expense that occurred, then Xero will help you to record, manage, claim, and reimburse the expense claims. You can also add expenses easily and attach the receipt images.

Xero has some great inventory management tools available for small businesses that do not offer services and instead sell merchandises that are kept in inventory. Here you can track your inventory and show how much inventory you have in stock.

As I mentioned with QuickBooks Online, it has limitations when it comes to mobile apps. Xero is one of these programs that allows for great mobile accessibility. The mobile app for Xero allows you to:

- Create and Send Invoices

- Add Receipts

- Attach Billable Expenses to Customer Invoices

- Submit Expense Reports

- Reconcile Transactions

- Access your Dashboard for Realtime View of your Cash Flow

- Use an additional app for Employees for Submitting Time Sheets, Request Time Off, and View Paystubs

One thing that sets Xero apart from other software is that it also has the capability to have a developer design and customize your own app by providing the API to allow for integration to your Xero account.

There is also a 24/7 customer support for those times that you have issues with your account, allowing you to have your books back up without losing the sale. However, there is one drawback to Xero. There are not many accountant and bookkeepers who know the software. Therefore, it brings in limitations to finding someone to keep your books.

**Zoho Books**

If you are a sole proprietor, freelancer or E-Commerce with a home-base business, then this is a great bookkeeping software for you. It is easy to use and affordable. It will allow you to connect with all your accounts and it covers all the basic needs of your business.

Zoho Books offer three pricing plans. The basic plan is $9 per month. This plan only supports one user and allows you to add 50 contacts. Other features include:

- Reconcile Transactions

- Create Invoices

- Track Expenses

- Manage Projects

- Manage Time Sheets

The standard plan is $19 per month and supports 2 users. It also allows for 500 contacts to be added. This plan includes:

- Reconcile Transactions

- Create Invoices

- Track Expenses

- Manage Projects

- Manage Time Sheets

- Track Bills

- Track Vendor Credits

- Add Reporting Tags to your Transactions

The professional plan is $29 per month and allows for 10 users. This plan also allows for unlimited contacts. It also includes:

- Reconcile Transactions

- Create Invoices

- Track Expenses

- Manage Projects

- Manage Time Sheets

- Track Bills

- Track Vendor Credits

- Add Reporting Tags to your Transactions

- Create Sales Orders

- Create Purchase Orders

- Manage Inventory

Zoho Books has one of the best customer services and support. The phones are open 24 hours a day, five days a week.

One disadvantage of Zoho Books is that it does not offer payroll services. If you have employees than you would need software that is for payroll. If you do not have employees then this is the best for you and your business.

**FreshBooks**

I mentioned earlier that there is software for bookkeeping that is great for those who want more accessibility through mobile apps. What makes FreshBooks the best is that you can find almost all the features in the mobile app that you have on the website. Keep in mind, if your business has inventory then this may not be the software for you.

Most all the software we have been talking about is based on features. With FreshBooks, the pricing is based on active clients.

For the Lite plan, it is $15 per month and allows you to bill up to five clients. The plus plan is $25 per month and allows you to bill up 50 clients. The premium plan is $50 and allows to bill up to 500 clients.

For each of the plans you can add contractors at no additional cost. However, if you need to add employees it is an extra $10 per month for each employee. Contractors and employees can view different parts of the books.

Employees can:

- View and Create Invoices and Expenses

- View the Dashboard

- Generate Reports

- Contractors can:

- View Projects they have been Assigned to

- Track Time towards the Assigned Projects

- Create and Send You Invoices for their Time

FreshBooks also has some timesaving features. You can create, send and manage invoices easily. This can be done from your computer or mobile app. It also allows for faster payments and makes tracking your expenses easy and allows for project management and time tracking.

With all software, customer service is a must. You will find both phone and email support. However, it is not 24/7 support. They do have hours between 8 a.m. to 8 p.m. eastern standard time Monday through Friday. With such great interface of mobile app then they also have support for those issues that may arise as well.

### Wave Accounting

That brings us to the last bookkeeping software we are going to look at, Wave Accounting. Wave Accounting is great if you do not have much equity to start with, as this software is free. Yes, that's right, I did say free.

Wave Accounting is designed for very small businesses with 10 employees or fewer and no inventory. If your business offers services, then you may want to try it out. If you plan on growing your business, eventually you will need to transition to another form of software.

Keep in mind, what keeps Wave Accounting free is the use of advertising. That means it will not only post advertising on the software while you use it, but it will also include its branding on your communications with customers.

You can also add credit card processing for small fee per transaction. The same goes for payroll processing as this can be added for $15 per month as well as an additional $4 per employee per month.

Keep in mind, Wave Accounting does still offer the basics for the needs of your company. With the advertising, if you want to have your business separated from all the ads, then you may want chose a different software such as Zoho Books.

## Create a Logo

One thing that will set your business apart from the rest is the business logo you create. This logo will be displayed on invoices, business cards, brochures, website, etc.

This should represent your business. You do not need to spend a lot of money on a good design. Search around and you will find a lot of sites that offer logo design for cheaper.

If you have some creative talent and want to create your own you can do that as well. A great place to start is through https://www.canva.com. This site is user friendly and free, although you do not need to use this site. You can easily create it in Word, Photoshop, Paint, etc. Make sure to save your logo as a JPG or PNG. If you use Word, then hit print screen and copy it into Paint so that you can save it in the proper format. Chose a good size for the logo and crop if needed. You may want to save different sizes as well. For example, you may have one size for your invoices, a size for your business cards, and a size for your letterhead when sending out emails and letters on behalf of the business.

## Monthly Bookkeeping Reports

Many times, businesses start to struggle because they do not know how the business is doing from the beginning. A good rule of thumb is to actively have the books up-to-date and always accurate. This will help when you do reports.

Also, make sure you are pulling the reports monthly. Do not just wait until the end of the quarter or year. If you have the reports each month it will give you a better understanding of how your business is doing and can help you make changes, if needed, for the following month.

With that said, I also want you to understand it is also just as important to do quarterly and yearly reports. This will help you judge how the business is doing overall throughout the year and throughout the years.

## Hire Employees

Adding employees to your business is not always the easiest to keep up with. It brings new responsibilities as you will need to keep track and pay their wages. One thing that can help with this is the bookkeeping software applications that we have discussed. It is worth ensuring you have the payroll feature if you have employees. Your employees rely on this paycheck.

Granted with payroll, you also have payroll taxes. This money belongs to the government. One thing that could help with this is to have a separate savings account within your business account for holding all the payroll taxes. That way when it comes time to pay the government the money is already set aside.

Make sure you are filing the correct documents for payroll on time otherwise you could encounter added fines.

## Try New Systems

There are so many systems out there that will help your business succeed. We have talked about a few of the software programs used for bookkeeping. However, if you add too many systems at once it could be overwhelming for you, your employees, and your customers.

As the business owner, you need to carefully select the applications you need for your business. A good rule of thumb is only try the systems that are needed for either maintenance or growth. If your business does not need it for either one of these, then do not add them! One thing that could help with this is having a website or mobile app designed that integrates everything you need for your business. You can add a feature that allows you, your employees, and your customers to access the same app, but based on their credentials they will only have access to what is needed for them.

Keep in mind, if you introduce one system at a time you will be able to give everyone a chance to learn the system before introducing the next.

## Be Hands-On with your Bookkeeper

As a business owner, you need to take a hands-on approach with your bookkeeper. In the starting phase, you might not afford to hire a bookkeeper and therefore must do it yourself or have one of your staff members do it. Always make sure you know what is going on with your accounts if you allow your staff to do the bookkeeping.

Bookkeeping is basic transactions, but you do need to see those reports each month, quarter, and year. If you record an invoice or expense in the wrong account the books can still balance but the accounts may not.

A bookkeeper needs to know and understand where all transactions will be recorded. I would also say the same about the business owner. If you are the business owner, you need to read the reports each month and know if something does not look right and needs to be reviewed. The same goes with the bookkeeper. If you are the bookkeeper, you need to go through all the transactions that were recorded that month to ensure that they were recorded in the correct account before the reports are generated.

One thing you could do is have a professional consultant bookkeeper look at the books for any errors. If you are worried about upsetting your bookkeeper, then add it to your company policy that a routine audit will be conducted at the end of each month or quarter.

## Outsource to a Bookkeeper

If you, as the business owner, is also the bookkeeper for an extended period of time, then you may want to outsource your bookkeeping. This can be the most cost effective as you are only paying for a couple hours of work. On the other hand, if you had an employee assigned to it, you are paying a monthly wage. You can also outsource to ensure that the books are being handled by a professional and will be accurate.

In general, it could take a professional bookkeeper only two to four hours to process an entire month of transactions and provide your business the monthly reports you require.

If you feel that you can handle some of the bookkeeping and only want the professional to handle specific areas you can do that as well.

One of the benefits of outsourcing to a professional is that they can give great business advice that will help your business grow. Some of this advice could be, but is not limited to:

- New software and if they would be a good fit for your business

- Attend business meetings with you and your banker

- Help with annual budget and cashflow reports

- Train office employees

# Chapter 3 – Managing Assets, Liabilities and Owner's Equity

Before we start to break down the financial reports, let's consider the management of the three areas of the accounting equations. Those are assets, liabilities, and owner's equity.

## Assets

Here are some assets to be aware of:

- The Credit and Debit Cards the Business Holds

- Loans that your company has made to others

- Money Market Accounts

- Brokerage Services

- Equipment

- Fixed Income

- Real Estate or Property

- Commodities and International Investments

Many businesses will need some kind of funding.  Therefore, when selecting a financial institution, you should know what the bank is looking at when deciding upon who to give a loan.

The following is a list of what most banks look for:

- Minimum Years in Business

- Minimum Revenue

- Minimum FICO Score: Does the loan require personal credit?

- Profitability: Does the loan require you to bring in a profit?

- Bankruptcy: Even if you have filed for bankruptcy, do you still qualify?

- Credit Card Volume: Some loans rely on credit card volume used by your business.  This is because those loans are paid off based on the volume.

- Accounts Receivable: Some alternative loans will consider your accounts receivable in their decision.

- Existing Debt: Do you have a debt with another lender?  If so, check to see what they require if you take out another loan.

A Small Business Administration Loan:

| **Years in Business Required** | 2+ years |
|---|---|
| **Revenue** | $50,000 |
| **Credit Score** | 640+ |

| Profitability Required | No |
|---|---|
| Bankruptcy Allowed | Yes! You could qualify with no less than 3 years after filing for bankruptcy. |
| Credit Card Volume Factored | No |
| Accounts Receivable Factored | No |
| Second Position Allowed for Debt | No! The SBA will not take a second position to another lender. |

Short-Term Loan:

| Years in Business Required | 6+ months |
|---|---|
| Revenue | $65,000+ |
| Credit Score | 500+ |
| Profitability Required | No |
| Bankruptcy Allowed | Yes! You could qualify with no less than 1 year after filing for bankruptcy. |
| Credit Card Volume Factored | In some cases. If it is, there is a minimum of $3,000+ |
| Accounts Receivable Factored | No |
| Second Position Allowed for Debt | In some cases |

Medium-Term Loan:

| Years in Business Required | 1+ year |
|---|---|
| Revenue | $150,000+ in most cases. Sometimes if only 1 lender they will consider $25,000+ |
| Credit Score | 600+ |
| Profitability Required | No |
| Bankruptcy Allowed | Yes! You could qualify with no less than 2 years after filing for bankruptcy. |
| Credit Card Volume Factored | No |
| Accounts Receivable Factored | No |
| Second Position Allowed for Debt | In some cases |

Line of Credit:

| Years in Business Required | 1+ year |
|---|---|
| Revenue | $200,000+ |
| Credit Score | 600+ |
| Profitability Required | Yes |
| Bankruptcy Allowed | Yes! You could qualify with no less than 2 years after filing for bankruptcy. |
| Credit Card Volume Factored | No |
| Accounts Receivable Factored | Yes |
| Second Position Allowed for | In some cases |

| Debt | |
|------|---|
| | |

Invoice Financing:

| Years in Business Required | 6+ months |
|---|---|
| Revenue | $50,000+ |
| Credit Score | 500+ |
| Profitability Required | No |
| Bankruptcy Allowed | Yes |
| Credit Card Volume Factored | No |
| Accounts Receivable Factored | Yes |
| Second Position Allowed for Debt | Yes |

Startup Loan:

| Years in Business Required | 0+ |
|---|---|
| Revenue | 0+ |
| Credit Score | 700+ |
| Profitability Required | No |
| Bankruptcy Allowed | Yes! You could qualify with no less than 3 year after filing for bankruptcy. |
| Credit Card Volume Factored | No |
| Accounts Receivable Factored | No |

| Second Position Allowed for Debt | No |
| --- | --- |

## Liability

We also need to look at the liabilities of the company. These can include things like customer deposits, fund securities, etc. It can be good to keep contact with a good financial advisor that can either handle or help you handle the assets and liabilities.

Although, most people who are just starting out cannot afford a financial advisor. No matter how good you are in business and keeping your business in control you will have some sort of liability.

However, you can ensure that your business and assets are protected from these liabilities that can arise.

We will briefly discuss how we can protect ourselves.

## Personal Liability:

Even though you incorporate or form a Limited Liability Company you may have personal liabilities. These are some circumstances that would be a personal liability:

- Person guarantee a loan for the business

- Your actions result in an injury

- You committed a crime or operated your business illegally

- You do not operate your business as if it's separate from your personal accounts.

## Business Liability Insurance:

To better help you protect yourself it is a very good idea to have business liability insurance. This will protect your small business from personal injury or property damage if a lawsuit arises. Here are the three types of business liability insurance:

- General Liability Insurance: Protects from injury claims, property damages, and claims of negligence and advertising claims.

- Product Liability Insurance: Protects against financial loss as a result of defective products that cause harm.

- Professional Liability Insurance: Protects business owners who provide a service. Protects against malpractice, errors, negligence, and omissions.

## Owner's Equity

There really is not a set way to manage the owner's equity. This is based off the investments from stocks, the money you put into the company, and the amount you withdraw from the company. For these types of transactions, you can use a regular business bank account and link it to your bookkeeping software.

# Chapter 4 – Using Ledgers and Journals to Track Business Activity

Before we can start to understand the financial reports, we need to look at where the information comes from. We can start with the journal entries that are made by the business and when those entries are posted to the ledgers. Next, we will then look at how we can track those transactions. Knowing where the transactions came from and where they are listed in the financial reports will help you better understand the reports that are created.

## Financial Journals

Most of the time when we talk about journaling in accounting and bookkeeping we refer to the General Journal.

How many times have you looked at the General Journal and gotten lost on how the business is really doing? Don't worry! If you said a lot or all the time then you are not alone. That is why in bookkeeping, along with the General Journal, you have six additional journals. They are:

1. Cash Receipts Journal (CRJ)

2. Cash Payments Journal (CPJ)

3. Sales Journal (SJ)

4. Sales Returns Journal (SRJ)

5. Purchase Journal (PJ)

6. Purchase Returns Journal (PRJ)

7. General Journal (GJ)

Let's look at each of the seven journals to get a better understanding. In the examples, you will also see the ref field. There may be references there that do not correspond to a journal. That is because they will correspond to a specific ledger. We will be talking about ledgers later in this chapter.

Remember, if you are using accounting software then all this is done for you through that software. However, it is nice to know the basics so that you can better understand where the financial reports are coming from.

## Cash Receipts Journal (CRJ)
When you receive cash, you will record it in the Cash Receipts Journal. The categories of the CRJ are:

- Date

- Details

- Ref.

- Bank

- Income

- Debtors

- Sundry

When you look at the CRJ, you will see three major categories: The bank is the total of each line and shows how much cash was received. Income is taken from receipts where you brought in money, while debtors is when you have a receipt where you paid out money. The category "sundry" is a word that means "various," miscellaneous," or "general."

Here is an example of a CRJ:

| DATE | DETAILS | REF | BANK | INCOME | DEBTORS | SUNDRY |
|------|---------|-----|------|--------|---------|--------|
| 1 | Capital | S1 | 15,000 | - | - | 15,000 |
| 7 | Loan | S2 | 5,000 | - | - | 5,000 |
| 12 | Service rendered | L1 | 10,500 | 10,500 | - | - |
| 30 | Smiths | L2 | 5,000 | - | 5,000 | - |
| | | | | | | |
| Total | | | 35,500 | 10,500 | 5,000 | 20,000 |

## Cash Payments Journal (CPJ)

Much like the CRJ, the Cash Payments Journal shows where the cash has been paid out of the business. The categories of the CPJ are:

- Date

- Details

- Ref.

- Expenses

- Creditors

- Sundry

- Bank

If you notice, the categories are the same except for income is now expenses, the Debtors is now Creditors, and the bank category is now at the end. Here is an example of a CPJ:

| DATE | DETAILS | REF | EXPENSES | CREDITORS | SUNDRY | BANK |
|------|---------|-----|----------|-----------|--------|------|
| 8 | Equipment purchased | A1 | - | - | 12,000 | 12,000 |
| | | | | | | |
| 9 | Drawings | S3 | - | - | 500 | 500 |
| 12 | Salary | E1 | 4,000 | - | - | 4,000 |
| 13 | Telephone company | L2 | - | 200 | - | 200 |
| 15 | Loan repayment | S4 | - | - | 4,000 | 4,000 |
| | | | | | | |
| Totals | | | 4,000 | 200 | 16,500 | 20,700 |

Keep in mind that if you prefer using a cash book, it is a combination of the SRJ and the SPJ. This will allow for the cash book to show all receipts and payments together.

If your business has a petty cash fund, you can keep track of this fund with additional journals and use the same format as the CRJ and the CPJ.

## Sales Journal (SJ)

Whether you're are offering services, merchandise, or both, I think we can agree that sales are important. That's why a Sales Journal is a great tool to have. Remember that only the income on credit will be recorded in the SJ. Once it is paid and your business receives cash for the service, then it will be recorded in the cash receipts journal.

The categories for the SJ:

- Date

- Debtor

- Ref.

- Services rendered

Here is an example of what a Sales Journal may look like:

| DATE | DEBTOR | REF | SERVICE RENDERED |
|------|--------|-----|------------------|
| 8 | Smiths | L2 | 5,000 |
| | | | |
| | | | |
| Total | | | 5,000 |

## Sales Returns Journal (SRL)

If you have a company that has merchandise, you occasionally deal with returned merchandise. You will use the Sales Returns Journal to track the returns that have been originally sold.

The categories within the SRL are:

- Date

- Debtor

- Ref.

- Sales returns

Here is an example of what an SRL may look like:

| DATE | DEBTOR | REF | SALES RETURNS |
|------|--------|-----|---------------|
| 16 | J. Jacobs | R1 | 300 |
| | | | |
| | | | |
| Total | | | 300 |

## Purchases Journal (PJ)

When your business has inventory, you will also have a Purchases Journal. This journal is used when your business purchases inventory on credit. Remember, a PJ only applies to inventory. Therefore, not all assets are recorded here. Only inventory purchased on credit will be recorded in the PJ.

The categories on a Purchases Journal are:

- Date

- Creditor

- Ref.

- Purchases

Here is what a Purchases Journal may look like:

| DATE | CREDITOR | REF | PURCHASES |
|------|----------|-----|-----------|
| 3 | J.P. Manufacturers | P1 | 5,500 |
| 5 | Wood Importers Inc. | P2 | 1,500 |
| | | | |

| | | | |
|---|---|---|---|
| Total | | | 7,000 |

## Purchases Returns Journal (PRJ)

Just like the SRJ, the Purchases Returns Journal is for recording merchandise that your business purchased on credit and then needed to return to the merchandise.

The categories for the PRJ are:

- Date

- Creditor

- Ref.

- Purchases returns

Here is an example of what a Purchases Returns Journal may look like:

| DATE | CREDITOR | REF | PURCHASES RETURNS |
|---|---|---|---|
| 3 | J.P. Manufacturers | P1 | 100 |
| 5 | Wood Importers Inc. | P2 | 1,500 |
| | | | |
| Total | | | 1,600 |

## General Journal (GJ)

So many times, we talk about the General Journal as it holds all the transaction a business makes. When you think about it, by using that definition of a general journal you are referring to all seven journals. However, the General Ledger does that very thing. That is right! The General Journal has all the transactions that do not fit into the other six journals.

The format is simple. It includes:

- Date

- Description

- Ref.

- Debit

- Credit

Here is an example of what a basic journal may look like:

| DATE | DISCRIPTION | REF | DEBIT | CREDIT |
|------|-------------|-----|-------|--------|
| Apr 2 | Description for the Debit | | 1,000 | |
| | Indent the description for the Credit(s) | | | 1,000 |
| | | | | |
| 16 | Description for the Debit | | 7,000 | |
| | Indent the description for the Credit(s) | | | 7,000 |
| | | | | |
| 19 | Description for the Debit | | 3,000 | |

| | Indent the description for the Credit(s) | | | 3,000 |
|---|---|---|---|---|
| | | | | |
| Totals | | | 11,000 | 11,000 |

When working with the general journal, always remember the Debits and Credits must equal.

# The Ledgers

For bookkeeping and double-entry accounting there are three main categories of ledgers we need to look at.

1. General Ledger (GL)

2. Accounts Receivable Ledger (ARL)

3. Accounts Payable Ledger (APL)

You may think that it is a waste of time to record the entries twice. You will find that just because you have journaled the transactions in one of the seven journals it is beneficial to organize the transactions into the ledger accounts as well.

## General Ledger (GL)

When you set up your business bookkeeping, a Chart of Accounts was created. Each account on this Chart of Accounts has a Ref number assigned to it. This reference comes in handy for both the Journals and the Ledgers. For each account on the Chart of Accounts you will have a General Ledger for the account. In each General Ledger, you will have either a Debit or Credit normal balance.

In the seven journals, you would record the ledger or associated journal in the ref field. In the ledgers, you will record the corresponding journal in the ref field.

Let's look at the General Journal for your business's Cash account.

Account: Cash - Ref: 100

| DATE | DESCRIPTION | REF | DEBIT | CREDIT |
|------|-------------|-----|-------|--------|
| Apr 1 | Opening Balance | | 4,500 | |
| 1 | | J1 | | 25.00 |
| 4 | | J1 | 180.00 | |
| 4 | | J1 | | 250.00 |
| 8 | | J2 | | 145.00 |
| 10 | | J2 | 25.00 | |
| | | | | |
| Total | Note: End of Month totals) | | 4,285 | |

The total is calculated at the end of each month and carried forward to the next month as the new opening balance. There will be a ledger for each account on the Chart of Accounts.

## Accounts Receivable Ledger (ARL) and Accounts Payable Ledger (APL)

The Accounts Receivable and Accounts Payable Ledgers are subsidiary ledger accounts. These are accounts that are in addition to the General Ledgers but are mainly for tracking the receivables and payables.

You may have multiple accounts of vendors who owe you money or you owe money too. Each account will have their own ledger.

Accounts Receivable will have a Debit normal balance while Accounts Payable will have a Credit normal balance.

Here is an example of each type of ledger:

Debtor: A. Franklin - Ref: AR-F

| DATE | | REF | DEBIT | CREDIT | BALANCE |
|------|------|------|--------|--------|---------|
| July 18 | Terms 60 days | SJ1 | 150.00 | | 150.00 |
| 27 | Terms 30 days | SJ1 | 190.00 | | 340.00 |

Creditor: Smiths Manufacturer - Ref: AP-S

| DATE | | REF | DEBIT | CREDIT | BALANCE |
|------|------|------|--------|--------|---------|
| July 14 | Terms 60 days | SJ1 | | 60.00 | 60.00 |
| 21 | Terms 30 days | SJ1 | | 100.00 | 160.00 |

# Tracking Transactions

Now that we have the journals and the ledgers, how do we track all the activity that is going on? It is simple. Look at the Ref column. The Ref column will show the link between the seven journals and the ledgers from the Chart of Accounts.

In addition to the journals and ledgers, you will note that the income statement (profit and loss statement) and the balance sheet will be constructed from the General Ledgers.

# Chapter 5 – Employees

Whenever you bring on new employees there are certain things that you need to look at. This is the basics of your payroll structure that is created for the business.

Now what is the plan? How are you going to gather what is needed for each new employee? Here are 10 steps that will help you establish this goal. We will talk about each step so you can successfully hire new employees.

1. Get an Employer Identification Number (EIN).

2. Find out whether you need state or local tax IDs.

3. Decide if you want an independent contractor or an employee.

4. Ensure new employees return a completed W-4 form.

5. Schedule pay periods to coordinate tax withholding for IRS.

6. Create a compensation plan for holiday, vacation and leave.

7. Choose an in-house or external service for administration payroll

8. Decide who will manage your payroll system.

9. Know which records must stay on file and for how long.

10. Report payroll taxes as needed on a quarterly and annual basis.

Filing and withholding taxes may seem stressful. It does not need to be. In fact, the IRS maintains an Employer's Tax Guide. This can be found on the IRS website at www.irs.gov. Search for Publication 15 (2017), (Circular E), Employer's Tax Guide.

# Get an Employer Identification Number (EIN)

If your business is about to hire employees as it is expanding, then you will need an Employer Identification Number (EIN). This number is a nine-digit number and will look like this: 12-3456789. It will be used for identifying the tax account of the employer. There are certain types of businesses that need an EIN who do not have employees. For this you can research the Employer's Tax Guide to find out if you need one or not.

There are two ways to apply for an EIN. The quickest is to apply through the IRS website at IRS.gov/ein. It will give you instructions and allow you to fill out the application electronically. The second is to fill out form SS-4, also found on the IRS website and fax or mail it to IRS. For both methods, be sure you have all the required information you need for the application. The best way is to find form SS-4 and fill that out before you fill out the online application. This way you have all the required information and can easily fill out the online application. Keep in mind, you will need to fill out the online application in one setting and it times out after 15 minutes of inactivity.

On the occasion that you bought someone's business, you will still need to file for your own EIN. This number is unique to the employer.

When it comes time to file your return and you do not have the EIN yet, file a paper return and write "Applied for 20 April 20XX" in the space shown for the number. Keep in mind, the date is the date you applied for the EIN.

All states have federal taxes that will need to be withheld. Your EIN is also known as your Federal Tax ID. A good rule of thumb is to apply for one as soon as you register your business.

## Find out whether you need state or local tax IDs

Your state may not require you to pay state taxes. There are seven states that do not have income taxes and an additional two who only impose tax if the income is from dividends.

The best way to know if you need a state tax ID is by visiting your states website.

## Decide if you want an independent contractor or an employee

A good question is if you are going to hire an independent contractor or an employee. This could determine how the taxes are withheld from the payroll.

Contractors will be operating under a different business name and will invoice you for the work. Keep in mind, there are times where a contractor can qualify as an employee in a legal sense. If you choose to hire contractors, you should get familiar with the Equal Employment Opportunity Commission Guide and the Fair Labor Standards Act.

## Ensure new employees return a completed W-4 form

Every employee must have a current W-4 on file with your business. This is needed so you can accurately dedicate taxes for your employees. So, make sure that each new employee files the W-4 with your business as part of the hiring process. The form can be found either on the IRS website or by Google searching for W-4.

1. The lines that need to be filled out are:

2. First and Last Name, Home Address, City, Stat, and ZIP

3. Social Security Number

4. Single, Married, or Married but withhold at higher single rate

5. Check if name is different than SS Card

6. Total number of Allowances

7. Additional amount to be withheld

8. Claim exemptions

The employee will sign and date the form. Line eight is for the employer and will include employer's name and address, office code, and EIN.

# Schedule pay periods to coordinate tax withholding for IRS

Most of us have worked for someone and you should have noticed that they had a set pay period. This makes it easy for your employees to know when they will be getting paid. Many employers have the pay period as every two weeks, while others, such as the military, have it on specific days. For instance, the military uses the 1st and the 15th of the month to pay their soldiers.

No matter what schedule you use, be consistent. Keep the same schedule for all employees and do not change it.

# Create a compensation plan for holidays, vacation and leave

There are many different plans that you need to consider now that you are going to have employees. Now, we are going to look at the compensation plan.

Does your business work on holidays? If so how are you going to pay your employees and how long will they work? When your employees work holidays, you need to pay those employees 1.5 per hour, also known as time and a half. Let's say the hourly rate is $10 and they worked 6 hours on a holiday that qualifies for holiday pay. They will get $60 for their shift plus $30 for the holiday. Therefore, for 6 hours on a holiday at $10 per hour you will pay your employee $90.

At the same time, if you offer vacation pay, sick pay, or emergency leave pay, then you will calculate that pay based off the hours they would have normally worked that day.

For the compensation plan you will withhold taxes like you normally would for their normal pay period.

# Choose an in-house or external service for administrating payroll

Making the decision to have your payroll done in-house or outsourced to another business can be one of the biggest decisions you will make for your businesses payroll. Here are a few questions you can ask yourself to help you make the decision a little easier. After all, the wrong decision for the payroll could cost you a lot of money.

1. How much control do you want over the process of paying your employees?

2. How frequently do your employees get paid?

3. Do different groups of employees get paid at different times?

4. How often do you have to give out last minute pay checks and changes?

5. How often do you process off-cycle payments?

6. How complicated is your payroll? Do you have employee benefits and deductions, allowances, etc.?

7. Does your organization have the resources to support an in-house payroll?

8. Do you have someone on your team that has a good understanding of payroll and statutory reporting?

9. How many accounts do you need to update on the general ledger?

10. Do you want a record of all payroll transactions and changes made?

These are only a few questions you may want to consider. Keep in mind, the longer an outside source needs to work on it the more money you need to pay them. If you can limit it to only a few hours a week, then it would be good to use an outside source and utilize your employee in another area of the business. However, if you feel that it will cost you more to pay an outside source due to the number of transactions that need to be done and it turns into a fulltime job, you may want to consider doing the payroll in-house.

# Decide who will manage your payroll system
Now that you have your payroll system set up, another big decision is deciding upon a manager for it. For a small business, you may want to outsource this work as it will not be much work in the beginning. As your business grows, it would be a good idea for you

to have an employee or yourself, as the business owner, to get trained on good bookkeeping practices.

# Know which records must stay on file and for how long

One problem that many small businesses face is the duration of keeping files. That is why I am adding it here. Some would suggest that you should keep tax information for the business forever. I would not advise this unless you have an iCloud service that meets the security requirements for safeguarding the business and employees' information. Besides, if you are a big company, that is a lot of storage space that you would need just for files.

The IRS can audit your tax records for 3 years and can extend that for 6 years.

- **Business Tax Returns:** Should be kept until IRS can no longer audit your tax returns. (6 years)

- **Payroll Tax Records:** This will include time sheets, wages, tax deposits, benefits and tips. (4 years of taxes are due or when you paid them. Whichever is the later date)

- **Current Employee Files:** (7 years after employee leaves business or 10 years if employee was involved in a work-related accident)

- **Job Application Information:** (3 years even if you do not hire the employee)

- **Ownership Records:** Includes business formation documents, annual meeting minutes. By-laws, stock-ledgers, and property deeds. Keep in mind, your business may not have all these documents. These documents will be anything you needed to form your business. (Retained Permanently)

- **Accounting Service Records:** This will include financial statements, check registers, profit and loss statements, budgets, general ledgers, cash books, and audit reports. (At minimum 7 years. I would recommend permanently as it will give you an outlook of how your business has grown.)

- **Operational Records:** This includes bank account statements, credit card statements, canceled checks, cash receipts, and check book stubs. (7 years)

I know it seems like a long time to hold onto these records. Keep in mind, you want to protect your business and keeping these records can safeguard your business when a problem may come up.

In today's world, everything is digital. You may want to invest in a server that meets the requirements needed to protect these files.

# Report payroll taxes as needed on a quarterly and annual basis

Now that you have employees, you will need to report the payroll taxes. The taxes that must be deposited to the IRS are the federal income tax withholdings, social security, and Medicare taxes for both the employer and employee.

There are two deposit schedules. They are monthly and semi-monthly. Before you start each calendar year, look at the Publication 15 on the IRS website to determine which payment schedule you are required to use.

You have probably noticed I have referenced Publication 15 a few times. I would advise saving the publication as it has a lot of information you will be referring to while running your small business. Another one, depending on what form you are using, will be Publication 51.

Publication 15 will be for forms 941, 944, and 945. For form 943 you will use Publication 51.

---

As the employer, you will be required to report wages, tips, and other compensation paid by using the required forms. You will also report the taxes either by filing out the paper form and sending it into the IRS or by e-filing through the IRS website.

Let's look at the different forms:

**Form 941 (Employer's Quarterly Federal Tax Form)**

- Filed Quarterly

- Any employer who withholds federal income tax or social security and Medicare taxes

**Form 943 (Employer's Annual Federal Tax Return for Agricultural Employees)**

- Filed annually if reporting agricultural wages

**Form 944 (Employer's Annual Federal Tax Return)**

- Only if you have received a written notice about the 944 programs

**Form 945 (Annual Return of Withheld Federal Income Tax)**

- Only if you are filing to report backup withholdings

**Form 940 (Employer's Annual Federal Unemployment (FUTA) Tax Return**

- Only if you pay FUTA tax

With state taxes, they will vary from state to state. Check with your local business administration for small businesses for more details with the state tax reporting.

With all this talk about filing the taxes throughout the year, we should also mention the taxes when filing at the end of the year and what needs to get done at that time. Every business who has employees will need to prepare W2's. Because there is so much to cover for filing taxes and getting your business ready at the end of the year, I added a special bonus chapter at the end. This chapter will be dedicated to you and your bookkeeper to prepare your business for tax season.

## Setting-Up Direct Deposit

Setting up direct deposit can be easy with the right tools. Many software programs have the feature to set up direct deposit. The nice thing is when you run your payroll and have your business bank account linked to the software, it will make it easier to get the payroll out each pay period.

You will need to get some basic information from the employee. Most banks will give them a form with all that information on it. Here is the basics of what you will need:

- Bank's Routing Number or ABA. It is a nine-digit number that is associated with the bank. Can be found on checks and the bank website.

- Checking / Savings Accounting Number

- Bank name and Address

There can be some cost to direct depositing the pay check. Some banks charge a transaction fee and per-check fee. Be prepared to handle this out of the business funds so that your employee gets what they earned.

## Employee Benefits

The benefits that you can offer your employees are what will entice them to stay with your business. There are some benefits that you are required to offer by law. However, there are many that are optional.

## Required Benefits

Let's look at the benefits you will be required to have:

- Social Security Taxes: All employers must pay the same rate of SS tax as the employees.

- Workers' Compensation: These are required through a commercial carrier, self-insured basis, or the State Workers' Compensation Program.

- Disability Insurance: Disability pay is required in in some states but not all. Check with your state if it is required.

- Leave benefits: Most leave benefits are optional. However, consult the Family and Medical Leave Act (FMLA) for those leave options that are required.

- Unemployment insurance: This varies from state to state. You may need to register with your state workforce agency.

## Optional Benefits

There are many optional benefits that you may want to consider. A big one is a retirement plan. Even though medical insurance is not required, you can offer different types of medical plans. This will allow your employee to get better coverage based on their needs.

### Incentive Programs

Offering incentive programs is another great way to reward your employees. Be creative and come up with some ways that would benefit your employees. Some ideas would be wellness programs, memberships, bonuses, discounts, etc.

If you are wanting to add incentives, make sure you add them to your employee's handbook. This way everyone knows what your business is offering. For accounting and bookkeeping purposes, you may want to consider a benefits administration software. This will make it easier when it comes time to keep the books.

**Federal and State Labor Laws**

The labor laws are very important, especially when it comes to hiring. There are specific guidelines when hiring veterans, foreign workers, household employees, child labor, and people with disabilities. This is only to name a few as there are many others.

For complete details about these different labor laws, consult the Department of Labor's federal and state law resources.

# Chapter 6 – Depreciation

Your small business may buy equipment that is supposed to last several years. However, over those years your equipment will lose some of its value.

For example, you buy a computer with Windows 7 for $575. Three years later your computer starts to break and you need to find parts. Over that time your depreciation went from $575 to about $50. At the same time, with as fast as technology is advancing you can no longer get parts. Now your depreciation of $50 is considered a recycling fee.

As you can see, over time your equipment will lose its value, and we need to calculate this into the bookkeeping. The depreciation can be an annual income tax deduction. It will be listed as an expense on the income statement. You can take advantage of this deduction by filing Form 4562 with your tax return. For more information about the Depreciation and requirements you must have, refer to Publication 946 (How to Depreciate Property).

For you to be able to claim a depreciation deduction there are a few guidelines that your property needs to meet.

- You must own the property. However, you can also depreciate capital improvements for property that you lease.

- The property must be used for business or to produce income. If you use the property for both business and personal you cannot deduct the property based on only business use of the property.

- The property must have a determined life span of more than one year.

However, even if you meet all the requirements of property deduction; you cannot deduct the following property:

- Any property that is placed in service and disposed the same year.

- Any equipment that is used to build capital improvements. You can add allowable depreciation on the equipment during the construction based on improvements.

- Certain term interests.

Most property can be depreciated. You can depreciate buildings, machinery, vehicles, furniture, and equipment. However, land cannot be depreciated. This is because you are expected to use the land for the lifetime of your business and it will never depreciate. However, the building on the land you operate your business from can be depreciated.

You will need to identify many items when filing taxes and using Form 4562 for the depreciation deduction. This is to ensure the proper depreciation of the property. These items include:

- Depreciation method for the property

- Class life of the asset

- Whether the property is "Listed Property"

- Whether you elect to expense any portion of the asset

- Whether you qualify for any "bonus" first year depreciation

- Depreciable basis of the property

How do we calculate depreciation? There are two different methods which we will discuss now: Book Depreciation and the Tax Depreciation.

# Book Depreciation

For the books, you will often hear of the book depreciation. This type is mainly for accounting and bookkeeping purposes. The goal for this type of depreciation is to match the cost of an asset with the revenue it earns over the period of its lifetime. The most common method for this type of depreciation is the straight-line method. This can be calculated in two ways.

- Annual Depreciation = (COST − Residual Value) / Useful Life

- Annual Depreciation = (COST − Residual Value) * Rate of depreciation

Let's look at each area so you will be familiar with the different terms.

- Cost: Original cost of the property or equipment.

- Residual Value: This is also known as the scrap value. What will be the value of the property or equipment at the end of its life-spam?

- Useful Life: This is the amount of time you plan on keeping and using the equipment before you dispose of it.

- Rate of depreciation: This is the percentage of the useful life-span that is used in an accounting period. This can be calculated as follows:

Rate of depreciation = 1 / Useful Life * 100%

# Tax Depreciation

There are many methods that you can use to calculate depreciation. Therefore, you do not need to stick to only one type. When it comes to taxes, the IRS likes the accelerated depreciation method the best. This method returns more of your money early in the asset's life. There are a few different methods you can use to get an accelerated depreciation.

- Declining Balance Depreciation = Rate * Net Book Value

For this formula let's look at what rate a book value are.

- Rate: This is a fixed rate and can be calculated as: (salvage Value / Cost)(1 / Years)

- Net Book Value: Original cost – accumulated depreciation to date on the asset

We also need to look at the double declining balance.

- Double Declining Rate = 2 / Useful Life

- Double Declining Balance Depreciation = Net Book Value * 2 / Useful life

With depreciation, make sure you keep your receipts. This will help your bookkeeper, accountant, and auditors check to make sure there are no mistakes before tax time and each month.

# Chapter 7 – Adjusting Entries

You will find that adjusting entries are very important for your small business. These are journal entries that turn your accounting records into accrual based accounting. Normally these entries are made prior to issuing the financial statements.

Many times, adjusting entries are for expenses. However, there are times that an adjusting entry is needed for revenue.

There are two scenarios that need an adjusting entry before the financial statements are issued.

- When nothing has been inputted into the accounting records for certain expenses or revenue, although those expenses or revenue did occur and need to be included in the current income statement and balance sheet for that period.

- When there has been an entry into the records, but the amount will need to be divided up between more than one accounting period.

## Asset Accounts

When you make adjusting entries, you assure that both the balance sheet and income statement are in check. This means that they need to be up-to-date based on the accrual basis of accounting.

---

A good way to begin is by examining and reviewing each balance on the balance sheet. Let's look at the following example and break it down. This will be based on the account balances before any adjustments are made.

The areas that we will be focusing on are the following:

- Cash - $1,800

- Accounts Receivable - $4,600

- Allowance for Doubtful Accounts - $0

- Supplies - $1,100

- Prepaid Insurance - $1,500

- Equipment - $25,000

- Accumulated Depreciation-Equipment - $7,500

# Joe's Parcel Services

## Preliminary Balance Sheet-before adjusting entries

## December 31, 2015

| ASSETS | | | LIABILITIES | |
|---|---|---|---|---|
| Cash | $ 1,800 | | Notes payable | $ 5,000 |
| Accounts receivable | 4,600 | | Accounts payable | 2,500 |
| Supplies | 1,100 | | Wages payable | 1,200 |
| Prepaid insurance | 1,500 | | Unearned revenues | 1,300 |
| Equipment | 25,000 | | Total liabilities | 10,000 |
| Accumulated dereciation | (7,500) | | | |
| | | | OWNER'S EQUITY | |
| | | | Joe John, Captial | 16,500 |
| Totl assets | $ 26,500 | | Total liabilities & Owner's Equity | $ 26,500 |

## Cash - $1,800

In the general ledger, the cash account has a balance of $1,800. However, before creating the balance sheet, I want you to ask yourself two questions.

1. Is $1,800 the true amount of cash?

2. Does it agree with what was figured based on the bank reconciliation?

In the case of our example the amount $1,800 is correct. However, if cash does not match with the bank reconciliation, adjustments will be needed to bring the balance sheet in check. Examples of this would be service charges, banking fees, and check printing charges. These entries would need to be entered into the cash account to ensure that it matches the bank statements.

## Accounts Receivable - $4,600

For this account, you may want to review any unpaid invoices. They are often found in the accounts receivable subsidiary ledger. For this we will assume that $4,600 is accurate for the amounts not yet paid.

The balance sheet needs to report all amounts. This is to include the money not yet paid but due to the business. The same goes for all revenue that has been billed.

careful review, we learned that $3,000 of services has been carried. This is dated as of December 31, although it will not be billed until January 10. In order to have that information on the December financial statements, you need to make an adjusting entry.

Remember, all entries will have at least a credit and a debit. The two accounts that are affected will be Accounts Receivable and Service Revenue. Accounts Receivable has a normal debit balance and is part of the balance sheet accounts. Service Revenues has a normal credit balance and is part of the income statement accounts.

The adjusting entry will look like this:

| Date | Account Name | Debit | Credit |
|------|--------------|-------|--------|
| Dec 31 2015 | Accounts Receivable | 3,000 | |
| | Service Revenues | | 3,000 |

When we look at the previous balance of $4,600 for accounts receivable and then make the adjusting entry of $3,000, the new balance for this account will be $7,600.

**Allowance for Doubtful Accounts - $0**

If you notice, this account is not listed on the balance sheet. That is because it has a $0 balance. It is common for accounts with a $0 balance to not appear on the balance sheet.

At one point your business may have accounts that are not collected for varies reasons. Instead of reducing the Accounts Receivable by issuing a credit on the ledgers you will report it in the Allowance for Doubtful Accounts.

Therefore, let's say $600 will not be collected. That means that $600 needs to be reported in the Allowance for Doubtful Account. There will be two accounts involved for this transaction. You will have Allowance for Doubtful Accounts found on the balance sheet. This account has a credit normal balance. The other account will be Bad Debts Expense found on the income statement. This account will have a normal debit balance.

The adjusting entry for this will be:

| Date | Account Name | Debit | Credit |
|------|--------------|-------|--------|
| Dec 31 2015 | Bad Debts Expense | 600 | |
| | Allowance for Doubtful Accounts | | 600 |

This transaction will give the Allowance for Doubtful Account a balance of $600.

As you go through the balance sheet, keep in mind which accounts will be affected and which accounts that are affected and whether they have a normal debit or credit.

You should take the time to see if you can figure out the remaining adjusting entries for the asset accounts. They are:

- Supplies - $1,100

    o Adjusting entry - $375 (Hint: The balance for supplies will be $725 and the accounts involved are Supplies and Supplies Expense)

- Prepaid Insurance - $1,500

    o Adjusting entry - $900 (Hint: The balance for Prepaid Insurance will be $600 and the accounts involved are Prepaid Insurance and Insurance Expense)

- Equipment - $25,000

o No adjusting entry

- Accumulated Depreciation-Equipment - $7,500

    o Adjusting entry - $1,500 (Hint: The balance for Accumulated Depreciation-Equipment will be $9,000 and the accounts involved are Accumulated Depreciation-Equipment and Depreciation Expense-Equipment)

# Adjusting Entries – Liability Accounts

As you review the accounts on the balance sheet, do not stop at the assets. The liability accounts need to be reviewed also. Check these accounts much the same way as the assets. See if you can record these transactions for the liability accounts.

- Notes Payable - $5,000

    o No adjusting entry needed

- Interest Payable - $0

    o Adjusting entry - $25 (Hint: The balance for the Interest Payable will be $25 and the accounts involved are Interest Payable and Interest Expense)

- Accounts Payable - $2,500

    o Adjusting entry - $1,000 (Hint: The balance for Accounts Payable will be $3,500 and the accounts involved are Accounts Payable and Repairs & Maintenance Expense)

- Wages Payable - $1,200

- o Adjusting entry - $300 (Hint: The balance of Wages Payable will be $1,500 and the accounts involved are Wages Payable and Wages Expense)

- Unearned Revenues - $1,300

  - o Adjusting entry - $800 (Hint: The balance for Unearned Revenues will be $500 and the accounts involved are Unearned Revenues and Service Revenues)

Keep in mind the normal balances for each account affected. Here is a list of all the accounts affected with their normal balances. As you do these adjusting entries and you do not know the normal balance for both transactions, figure out which one you do know. There will always be a debit and a credit for each transaction made. If it has a credit normal balance and the adjustment increases the account, then you will debit the other account.

- Accounts Receivable – Normal Debit Balance

- Service Revenues – Normal Credit Balance

- Allowance for Doubtful Accounts – Normal Credit Balance

- All Expenses – Normal Debit Balance

- Supplies – Normal Debit Balance

- Prepaid Insurance – Normal Debit Balance

- Accumulated Depreciation-Equipment – Normal Credit Balance

- Interest Payable – Normal Credit Balance

- Accounts Payable – Normal Credit Balance

- Wages Payable – Normal Credit Balance

- Unearned Revenues – Normal Credit Balance

- Service Revenues – Normal Credit Balance

Remember, all the accounts that will be affected for the adjusting entries will come from the balance sheet and the income statement.

# Chapter 8 – Making Sense out of the Financial Statements

As a small business owner, you need to understand these basic statements so you will have a good outlook at where your business stands financially. This is where it is extremely important to communicate with your bookkeeper.

There are many financial statements that you could look at, depending on what you want to see. The basic statements we are going to look at are:

1. The Balance Sheet

2. The Income Statement

3. The Statement of Owner's Equity

4. The Statement of Cash Flow

These are also considered the BIG 4. The reason these are the big 4 is because they will give you a great understanding of where your business is financially. They are also the financial statements that investors use to make decisions and envision where your business could be in the future.

## The Balance Sheet

The balance sheet is a good example of the accounting equation.

- Assets = Liabilities + Equity

Within this financial statement you will see the three areas divided up to show what accounts are listed under Assets, Liabilities, and Owner's Equity. The owner's equity represents retained earnings for your business. You will see all accounts on the balance sheet that do not have a $0 balance. Generally, accounts with a $0 balance do not need to be displayed.

There are two types of formats that will be used for a balance sheet. You will have the vertical or horizontal formats. You saw a horizontal format in the previous chapter.

Most business prefer the vertical format. However, the horizontal format has a better understand of the accounting equation. Let's look at the example from the last chapter.

| ASSETS | | LIABILITIES | |
|---|---|---|---|
| Cash | $ 1,800 | Notes payable | $ 5,000 |
| Accounts receivable | 4,600 | Accounts payable | 2,500 |
| Supplies | 1,100 | Wages payable | 1,200 |
| Prepaid insurance | 1,500 | Unearned revenues | 1,300 |
| Equipment | 25,000 | Total liabilities | 10,000 |
| Accumulated dereciation | (7,500) | | |
| | | OWNER'S EQUITY | |
| | | Joe John, Captial | 16,500 |
| Totl assets | $ 26,500 | Total liabilities & Owner's Equity | $ 26,500 |

From this example, I want you to keep in mind the accounting equation: Assets = Liabilities + Owner's Equity. If you notice, the balance is split in two sections and these sections are put side-by-side. On one side you have the Assets of $26,500. On the other side you have the liabilities of $10,000 and the Owner's Equity of $16,500. Let's take the liabilities and the owner's equity. Add those together and you will get $26,500.

With that in mind, let's put the accounting equation into the balance sheet. Left side: $26,500 (Assets) = Right side: $10,000 (Liabilities)

+ $16,500 (Owner's Equity).  Now to see it more clearly you will have Left Side: $26,500 (Assets) = Right Side $26,500 (Liabilities + Owner's Equity).

Now what does this mean for your business?  Based on your business's assets, the business is balanced in its financial obligations. This is to include investments and retained earnings.

You can think of it this way.  Assets are the means a business uses to operate.  On the other hand, the liabilities and owner's equity are the two ways you support the assets.

Now that we have an understanding of the balance sheet, what about the accounts that are listed in each section?  It is important to know what accounts are asset, liability, and owner's equity.

## Current Assets

These assets will have a life span of less than one year.  This means they can be converted into cash.  They include:

- Cash and Cash Equivalents

    o Cash

    o U.S. Treasuries

- Accounts Receivable

    o Sort-Term obligations owed to the business by the clients

- Inventory

    o Raw materials

## Non-Current Assets

These assets cannot be turned into cash as easily. They are expected to be turned into cash within one year or have a life span of more than a year. Depreciation is usually calculated on these assets. Examples of these assets are:

- Tangible Assets

  o Machinery

  o Computers

  o Buildings

  o Land

- Intangible Assets

  o Goodwill

  o Patents

  o Copyright

**Liabilities**

When you look at the liabilities you should consider this as the obligations a business owes to others. Just like assets, they can be both current and long-term.

- Current Liabilities

  o Paid within one year

  o Accounts Payable

- Long-Term Liabilities

- o Debts that are more than one year

- o Non-Debts that are more than one year

**Owner's Equity**

This is the money that is invested in the business. The retained earnings from the income statement will also be transferred into the owner's equity at the end of the fiscal year. The owner's equity shows the net worth of your business. Types of accounts listed in the owner's equity:

- Capital – Money invested or earned by the business

- Drawing – Money that is withdrawn from the business

# The Income Statement

To a business owner the income statement may look scary. However, it does not need to be. The income statement takes a closer look at the revenue or sales and the expenses of the business. This is usually done on a quarterly and annually basis throughout the fiscal year.

You may hear terms such as profits, earnings, and income when talking about the income statement. Keep in mind, they all mean the same thing.

There are two basic formats that you will use, the multi-step and the single-step formats. Here are the steps for each format:

- Multi-Step Format

  - o Net Sales

  - o Cost of Sales

  - o Gross Income*

- o Selling, General and Administrative Expenses (SG&A)

- o Operating Income*

- o Other Income & Expenses

- o Pretax Income*

- o Taxes

- o Net Income (after tax)*

- Single-Step Format

  - o Net Sales

  - o Materials and Production

  - o Marketing and Administrative

  - o Research and Development Expenses (R&D)

  - o Other Income & Expenses

  - o Pretax Income

  - o Taxes

  - o Net Income

In the multi-step format there are four measures of profitability (*). Here is an example of an income statement:

| | 2015 | 2016 |
|---|---|---|
| Net Sales | 1,500,000 | 2,000,000 |
| Cost of Sales | (350,000) | (375,000) |
| Gross Income | 1,150,000 | 1,625,000 |
| Operating Expenses (SG&A) | (235,000) | (260,000) |
| Operating Income | 915,000 | 1,365,000 |
| Other Income (Expenses) | 40,000 | 60,000 |
| Extraordinary Gain (Loss) | - | (15.,000) |
| Interest Expense | (50,000) | (50,000) |
| Net Profit Before Taxes (Pretax Income) | 905,000 | 1,360,000 |
| Taxes | (300,000) | (475,000) |
| Net Income | 605,000 | 885,000 |

Once you know how the income statement is formatted and what is involved, you can see that between 2015 and 2016, there was an increase in sales by 33%. At the same time, the cost of sales was reduced from 23% to 19% in sales. If you look further you can see other increases and decreases between the two years.

## Statement of Owner's Equity

The Statement of Owner's Equity can be used as a separate statement or it can be included in the balance sheet and income statements. It is also known as a Statement of Retained Earnings. This statement will show the stands of your businesses earnings.

Many times you will see this more with corporations as they have shareholders and pay out dividends. However, it can be a useful tool for a small business to show your retained earnings and financial standings.

The main purpose for this statement is to release financial information to the public, so they can decide if they want to invest into your business. It will also help analyze the health of your business.

Here is an example of a Statement of Owner's Equity.

Alex Printing and Design

Statement of Owner's Equity

For the Year Ending December 31, 2015

Alex, Capital: $100,000

Add: Additional Contributions: $10,000

Net Income: $57,100

Total: $167,100

Less: Alex, Drawings: $20,000

Alex, Capital – Dec. 31, 2015: $147,100

# Statement of Cash Flow

One thing that is important is the flow of cash in and out of the business. The Statement of Cash Flow provides you with those answers. However, it is split up into four parts.

1. **Operating Activities** – This converts items that are on the income statement from the accrual basis of accounting to cash.

2. **Investing Activities** – This reports purchases and sales from long-term investments, property, plant and equipment.

3. **Financing Activities** – This reports issuance and repurchases of company bonds and stock as well as payments of dividends.

4. **Supplemental Information** – This reports exchanges of significant items. These items did not involve cash and will report the amount of income taxes and interests that are paid.

What is usually listed in each section? Let's take a look:

1. Operating Activities

   a. Accounts Receivable

   b. Inventory

   c. Supplies

   d. Prepaid Insurance

   e. Other Current Assets

   f. Notes Payable

   g. Accounts Payable

   h. Wages Payable

   i. Payroll Taxes Payable

   j. Interest Payable

   k. Income Taxes Payable

l.  Unearned Revenues

m. Other Current Liabilities

2. Investing Activities

    a.  Long-term Investments

    b.  Land

    c.  Buildings

    d.  Equipment

    e.  Furniture & Fixtures

    f.  Vehicles

3. Financing Activities

    a.  Notes Payable (generally due after one year)

    b.  Bonds Payable

    c.  Deferred Income Taxes

    d.  Preferred Stock

    e.  Paid-in Capital in Excess of Par-Preferred Stock

    f.  Paid-in Capital from Treasury Stock

    g.  Retained Earnings

    h.  Treasury Stock

4. Supplemental Information

Here is an example of a Statement of Cash Flow.

Frank's Deal LLC

Statement of Cash Flows

For Month Ended July 31, 2017

**Operating Activities**

Net Income: $100

Add back: Depreciation expense: $20

Add back: Loss on sale of equipment: $180

Increase in Inventory: ($200)

Increase in supplies: ($150)

Cash provided (used) in operating activities: ($50)


**Investing Activities**

Purchase of office equipment: ($1,100)

Proceeds from sale of office equipment: $900

Cash provided (used) or investing activities: ($200)


**Financing Activities**

Investment by owner: $2,000

Net increase in cash: $1,750

Cash at the beginning of the year: $0

Cash at July 31, 2017: $1,750

Knowing these four main financial statements will give you all the information you need for your business. These are the tools it takes to know the health of your business and plan for the future.

We have only touched base on the main financial statements. However, there are so many other reports you have access to. The main forms will give you all the financial information you will need to do ratios to see what the outcome of the business is. You can also compare the current years to see how the business has done from year-to-year.

# Chapter 9 – Taxes for Small Businesses

A huge part of bookkeeping is preparing the books for tax season. That is why, as a bonus, I am adding this chapter about taxes for small businesses.

If you are just starting, you may feel overwhelmed at tax time. You should not need to feel this way. As long as you keep your records up-to-date, it should be a breeze when it comes time for taxes.

I want to share this checklist with you. This is a list of items that you will need when it is time to file your taxes for the business.

**Income**

- Gross receipts from sales or services

- Sales records (for accrual based taxpayers)

- Returns and Allowances

- Business checking/savings account interest (1099-INT or statement)

- Other Income

**Cost of Goods Sold (if applicable)**

- Inventory

- Beginning inventory total dollar amount

- Inventory purchases

- Ending inventory total dollar amount

- Items removed for personal purposes

- Materials & Supplies

**Expenses**

- Advertising

- Phones (landlines, fax or cell phones related to business)

- Computer & internet expenses

- Transportation and travel expenses

  o Local transportation

    - Business trip (mileage) log

    - Contemporaneous log or receipts for public transportation, parking, and tolls

  o Travel away from home

    Airfare or mileage/actual expense if drove

    Hotel

    Meals, tips

    Taxi, tips

    Internet connection (hotel, internet café, etc.)

Other

- Commissions paid to subcontractors

  o File Form 1099-INT-MISCand 1096 as necessary

- Depreciation

  o Cost and first date of business use of asset

  o Records related to personal use of assets

  o Sales price and disposition date of any assets sold

- Business Insurance

  o Casualty loss insurance

  o Error and omissions

  o Other

- Interest Expense

  o Mortgage interest on building owned by business

  o Business loan interest

  o Investment expense and interest

- Professional fees

  o Lawyers, accountants, and consultants

- Office supplies

- o  Pens, paper, staples, and other consumables

- Rent Expense

  - o  Office space rent

  - o  Business-use vehicle lease expense

  - o  Other

- Office-in-home

  - o  Square footage of office space

  - o  Total square footage of home

  - o  Hours of use, if operating an in-home daycare

  - o  Mortgage interest or rent paid

  - o  Homeowner's or renters' insurance

  - o  Utilities

  - o  Cost of home, separate improvements and first date of business use

- Wages paid to employees

  - o  Form W-2 and W-3

  - o  Federal and state payroll returns (Form 940, Form 941, etc.)

      Employee benefit expense (This is to be aligned with "Wages paid to employees")

Contractors

Form 1099-MISC

Form 1096

- Other Expenses

  o Repairs, maintenance of office facility, etc.

  o Estimated tax payments made

  o Other business-related expenses

    Health insurance (Needs to be aligned with "Other expenses")

    Premiums paid to cover the sole-proprietor and family

    Premiums paid on behalf of partners and S corporation shareholders

    Information on spouse's employer provided insurance

I know this is a long list. It will ensure you and your bookkeeper are prepared. If you take the time each month to keep these documents organized and safe, when it comes time for taxes you will not need to look through everything to find what you need.

I encourage you to keep your business organized and in good shape. Make sure you keep your personal finances separate from your business finances. This includes separate bank accounts.

Before it is time to prepare for tax time, you should review the accounts receivable and inventory balances. This should be done at least quarterly. However, you should do it every time before closing the books and preparing them for the next fiscal year. Also make sure you review all equipment purchases for the year.

Many times there are added or potential tax credits you may be eligible for. Here is a list of just a few, but you would want to check and see what credits you could get each year as they could change.

- Research and Development Credit

- Energy Tax Credit

- Disabled Access Credit

- Work Opportunity Tax Credit

- Healthcare Tax Credit

Of course, as you close the books you will make your adjusting entries and prepare your business for the upcoming year.

For more information with filing taxes for your small business you can check out the IRS website at: https://www.irs.gov/businesses/small-businesses-self-employed

## Other Tax Deductions

As you may or may not know, when it comes to tax deductions for running your small business there are so many to think about. I compiled a list of some other types of deductions for you to consider.

- Employees' Pay – This can be deducted as long is the pay is in the form of cash, property, or services.

- Inventory (cost of Goods Sold) – If your business manufacture products or purchases products for resale you can deduct the cost of goods sold.

- Employee Benefits – Such benefits like healthcare, adoption assistance, education assistance, and life insurance can be deducted.

- Home Office – Make sure you have a dedicated room for your home office. You will need to calculate the square footage so that you can apply a percentage of your rent, mortgage, insurance, utilities, housekeeping, etc. That percentage can be deducted if you work out of your home.

- Auto Maintenance and Mileage – There are two ways to calculate this rate. You can use the standard mileage rate or the actual expenses paid. Be sure to use whichever gives you the greatest deduction.

- Advertising and Marketing – You can deduct the cost for marketing and advertising your business. This includes promotion costs for good publicity.

- Office Supplies – This can be anything you use for your office. Make sure you keep your receipt of all items. These are small day-to-day items.

- Education – This includes educating people about your business through seminars and trade shows. Also, if you have magazines, books, CD's and DVD's that relate to your business, they are 100% deductible.

- Professional Fees – This includes accountant, lawyer and consulting fees. They are 100% deductible.

- Travel Expenses – When the travel is business related it is mostly all 100% deductible. This includes airfare, hotels, and other road expenses. However, eating out can be deducted but only at 50%.

- Entertainment – This one can be tricky. If you are just going out with co-workers it is not deductible. However, if you bring a client or prospective client you can deduct 50%. Same goes for if you take them out for drinks as long as it is in a business setting or business meeting.

- Furniture – This is supposed to have a long lifespan. Therefore, you can either deduct the full cost of the furniture at one time or you can deduct the depreciation over several years.

- Office Equipment – This will be those big items such a fax machine, copier, or computer. They are also 100% deductible and can be deducted the same way as the furniture.

- Employee or Client Gifts – It is always nice to reward your employees or clients with a gift. These are 100% deductible up to $25 per year for each person.

- Startup Expenses (Capital Expenses) – You can deduct up to $5,000. This includes research costs that you incurred for creating your business.

- Taxes – That's right. Taxes that incurred through running your business can be deductible.

- Insurance Premiums – The credit, liability, malpractice, and workers' compensation premiums call all be deducted.

- Interest – The interest that you incur from mortgage, finance charges such as credit cards, payment plans, and interest on loans are 100% deductible.

- Software – This includes boxed, downloadable, and subscriptions. They are all deductible.

- Charitable Contributions – If the contribution is more than $250 you will need a letter from the organization verifying the contribution. If the donation is not money, you can visit the IRS website and look up Publication 561 - Determining the Value of Donated Property.

- Rent – If you rent and the property is used for your business you can deduct the rent. However, if you receive any of that rent as equity you are not able to deduct it.

- Freelancers – When you hire an independent contractor you can deduct their pay as a business expense.

- Repairs and Maintenance – When you run a business there will always be some repairs and maintenance that needs to be done for your business to still run smoothly. These are deductible.

- Licenses – License fees and regulatory fees are deductible.

- Etc. – There is so many more. With a little research, you could find deductions that you never knew existed.

## Preparing W-2's for your employees

Many times when we start a business and have employees we do not know how to prepare the W-2's. That is why I want to set you up for success in this area. When an employee first starts working with your business, you need to have them file a W4 for employee or a W9 for independent contractor. This is the basis for starting the W-2 preparations.

Let's first start by checking all the information on the W-4. This form needs to be on file with your business at all times. If there are any changes that need to be made, such as an employee moved, then you will need them to file an updated form. To ensure that all the information is correct before preparing the W-2 it is a good idea to have all employees look over their W-4 to ensure it is up-to-date. This form changes each year. Therefore, in January you must provide this form to all your employees for the current year.

**Gathering Information**

Let's look at some of the basic information you will need from your business for each employee.

- Business Employee ID Number

- Name, Address, and Zip Code of the business

- Business State Tax ID Number

This information will be on every W-2 prepared by the business. It is a good idea to have it saved where you can find it easily whenever it is needed.

Now we need to gather information about each employee.

- Employee name, address, and social security number or other tax ID number

- Amount paid to the employee. (i.e. total wages, tips, and other compensation)

- Amount of federal income tax withheld

- Social security wages (only up to the maximum amount for the year)

- Medicare wages and tips and Medicare tax withheld

- Allocated tips paid

- Dependent care benefits paid and benefits taxable to the employee

- State wages, tips, and income taxes withheld for each state the employee worked

- Local wages and tips paid and local income tax withheld

**Review and Creating your W-2's**

Keep in mind, every employee who worked for you during the year must get a W-2 from the business. This includes if they only worked for you one day. They will still receive a W-2.

There are many ways you can get the W-2 forms needed for printing. You can buy them from your local office supply store, your CPA, a tax or accounting software, and from the IRS. However, W2's are not downloadable from the IRS website.

There are a few options for printing your W-2 forms.

- Accounting Software – you may need to purchase an add-on for this processing feature

- Tax preparation Software – check to see if it is included with the software you are using.

- Purchase W2 forms

If you are able to, it is easier to use accounting software with the payroll feature. Simply get the add-on and all the work is done for you. Your accounting software will keep track of all the information for you and at the end of the year you will need to review to make sure it is accurate before printing.

Regardless of which method you use, you should also have a W-3 transmission form. A W-3 must be submitted to the IRS, which will show the totals of the W-2's.

### Distribution of the W-2's

Many businesses have different ways of distributing the W-2's. Remember, all W-2's must be out no later than January 31st.

There are two ways that W-2's can be distributed. You can choose to either mail them or have the employee pick them up. However, many businesses are making the W-2 more accessible on a secured business website. This allows employees to print out their own W-2 for filing taxes. It also helps to ensure employees will not lose their W-2 and need a copy from the employer.

### Filing W-2 and W-3 Forms

Now that you have gotten all of your W-2's out to the employees, it is time to decide how you are going to file them with the Social Security Administration. You will need to file form W-3 complete with copy A of each W-2 for your employees.

There are two ways to file these forms.

1. File online at the business services online section of the Social Security website. You will need to register first to file electronically.

2. Mail completed forms W-2 and W-3 to the Social Security Administration.

Also, if the employee pays state taxes, then copy 1 of the W-2 will get sent to the state taxing authority for every state they worked in and paid taxes to.

# Chapter 10 – Small Business Checklist

So many times we ask ourselves, "What do we need to do? When do we need to do it?" That is what this chapter will help us answer. Here is a checklist that will help your bookkeeper know when to perform each task to help you run your business smoothly.

**Daily Bookkeeping Tasks:**

- Check Cash Position

    o Cash is like the fuel to your company. Therefore, you never want to run out of cash to operate your business with.

**Weekly Bookkeeping Tasks**

- Record Transactions

- Document and File Receipts

- Review Unpaid Bills From your Vendors

- Pay Vendors and Sign Checks

- Prepare and Send Invoices

- Review Projected Cash Flow

**Monthly Bookkeeping Tasks**

- Balance the Business Checkbook

- Review Past-Due ("Aged") Receivables

- Analyze Inventory Status

- Process or Review Payroll and Approve Tax Payments

- Review Actual Profit and Loss vs. Budget vs. Prior Years

- Review Month-End Balance Sheet vs. Prior Period

## Quarterly Bookkeeping Tasks

- Prepare/Review Revised Annual P&L Estimate

- Review Quarterly Payroll Reports and Make Payments

- Review Sales Tax and Make Quarterly Payments

- Compute Estimated Income Tax and Make Payment

## Annual Bookkeeping Tasks

- Review Past-Due Receivables

- Review Inventory

- Fill Out IRS Forms W-2 and 1099-MISC

- Review and Approve Full-Year Financial Reports and Tax Returns

This checklist is only an example. With it, you can get started and on your way to becoming organized. As your business progresses and you meet with your bookkeeper, you may want to add to or take away from this checklist. It is here to act as a guide.

As you perform these tasks weekly, monthly, quarterly, or annually you may want to change it and perform some tasks more frequently. Sometimes when you are first starting out it is a good idea to run reports on a monthly basis. This will give you a better understanding of how you are doing each month.

# Chapter 11 – Bookkeeping tips for your Small Business

I want to take a few minutes to go over a few tips that you can follow. These tips will not only make things easier for you, as the business owner, but your bookkeeper will have an easier time as well.

Bookkeeping does not need to feel like a nightmare. With a little planning, you can have your records accurate and complete at all times.

## Tip 1: Keep Accurate Records

Most of your day-to-day business activities are handled and tracked through your online banking. However, the most important aspect is that your financial records are all kept in one place. This way you do not need to scramble to meet requests.

Granted, online banking will make it simple to track debits and credits. This does not mean you do not need some sort of bookkeeping records. It is important to know how the money was spent. Therefore, the records need to track the inflow and outflow of cash. This includes purchases with a credit card, when reimbursements are made to employees, etc.

Making a good investment in a cash basis accounting software will help with this tracking system.

## Tip 2: Sort and File Receipts

In your business, you will have a lot of receipts on a daily or monthly basis. Do not throw these away. However, filing them can be stressful. Keep in mind, if you file them and keep them organized it will eliminate the headaches in the future. It is vital that you keep all receipts for your business, although receipt accounts go well beyond just keeping the receipts.

Keep your receipts organized. Over time the ink on the receipts will fade. That's why it can be good to photocopy or scan your receipts. Then organize them by date to correspond with your detailed financial records. Many bookkeeping software will allow for you to scan and attach the receipt to the transactions made. This is a great feature that will help you keep track of all the receipts. However, even if the receipt is attached, you should still keep the scanned copy in case something happens with the software or it does not upload properly.

When keeping all your receipts, it will help reduce the headaches of tax time. If any of your items are tax deductible, you will need these receipts. Therefore, you should highlight the date and make notes about the reason for the expense. If you photocopy the receipt you will have room to make all the notes on the page with the receipt.

# Tip 3: Collect Applicable Taxes

I cannot stress this enough. Taxes need to be taken out at the time of the sale or when payroll is generated. Just like with the receipts, the longer you go between the transactions, the more chances for errors. Be sure to take care of the taxes when they occur.

You need to collect or apply taxes as soon as they occur, such as when a sale is made or payroll is generated. This will ensure:

1. Your business is not liable for a lump sum of taxes at the end of the year, and

2. Your business will not incur penalties due to delayed tax payments.

That's right. If the taxes are delayed after they incur, then the IRS will charge you a late penalty.

## Tip 4: Do Accurate Invoicing

Even though invoices are to let your clients know when to make payments, there is much more to it than that. An invoice is a record of terms of a transaction. Because of this, it is important that the information is accurate and complete. There is a difference between an invoice and a receipt. An invoice is what you will give to your clients letting them know how much and when to make payments to your business. You can also consider these as future inflows of cash. Receipts are your business expenses, or the outflows of cash.

## Tip 5: Get Donation and Contribution Receipts

There are tax benefits in donating to outside organizations, although to take advantage of these tax benefits you will need to get a receipt for verification of the donation. Each receipt should have how much the donation is worth.

There are some donations that require more than a check to ensure their validity. If the donation is over a specific amount, then a receipt is required.

Requesting a receipt seems like a simple request. Remember, that receipt could mean the difference between a tax write-off or the write-off being denied.

When in doubt, get a receipt. In this way you will always be covered for your contribution.

## Tip 6: Schedule Profit and Loss Statements

A great way to check the health of your company is a Profit and Loss Statement. This statement will provide an overview of many areas of the business. It can help summarize the business activity for a given period. That means you can have a P&L scheduled monthly, quarterly, or annually. It depends on the direction of your business.

Your bookkeeper or accountant may find discrepancies in the P&L as each one is pulled. It is important to have these printed to give them an idea which period of time that discrepancy occurred so that it can be corrected.

The P&L can also be key to finding and deciphering other records that you keep for your business.

These six helpful tips are a great way to make it easier for your business and bookkeeper. Some of the simplest tasks can be the most important. It will make it easier to perform each of these tasks if you follow a standard schedule of tasks to remind you of what needs to be done and when.

Proper and responsible time management of any task is the key ingredient for success. This is especially true in bookkeeping and accounting. Most of that scary feeling and large bit of time comes from poor preparation. Keep your business records accurate and organized on a daily basis. This will eliminate so much frustration along the way.

# Conclusion

This book has given you the tools to better understand not only your bookkeeper, but your business as well. These are all areas that you, as a business owner, need to know and understand.

Each area that we have covered has a purpose. When you work hand-in-hand with your bookkeeper, you will see the light at the end of the tunnel.

I mentioned in the beginning, "It is not the business owner that runs the business. It is the business owner teamed up with the bookkeeper that truly runs the business."

I want to take a minute to breakdown that statement. As the business owner, you have the power to make the decisions that will move your business forward. Your business will succeed or fail based on your decisions.

Your bookkeeper is the gate keeper. They hold the power over the financial health of your business. With their mighty power, you can have all the financial statements you need when you need them. They can also ensure that all the transactions are correct.

As a team, you are unstoppable. Your bookkeeper can ensure you have what is needed to move your business in the right direction. They can also help guide you in making the right decisions. With the proper analysis and ratios, you can predict the future if the trend is steady.

Now I have empowered you to be on the same level as your bookkeeper and accountant.

If you have not started your business yet, but you are thinking about it and currently doing the research for your business, then this is a great place to start.

With the knowledge that you have learned, you will also be better prepared to add your financials to your business plan and pitch deck.

Best of luck to all your endeavors. I look forward to seeing your business up and running and hearing about the great success you will be having.

Greg Shields

# Preview of Accounting

## The Ultimate Guide to Accounting *for Beginners –*
## *Learn the Basic Accounting Principles*

# Introduction

This book is intended for people who want to know something about the fundamentals of financial accounting without becoming an accountant. Many people are in this position; small business owners, employers, employees, business owners, stockholders, investors, and many, many more. Most of these folks do not need a deep understanding of accounting, they just need to learn what accounting is and how they should be using it. Just as important, they need to understand what accountants are talking about in their reports. They must learn the vocabulary and the most important terms. The product of accounting is information, important information for that wide range of stakeholders.

We will examine this subject in some detail, discussing accounting fundamentals, the various areas where accounting professionals work and the information they produce. We will also examine the measures and ratios that accountants use to analyze an organization's performance and the important relationship between time and money. The fact that information is the product of accounting will remain foremost in this book.

# Chapter 1 - Accounting is Different From Bookkeeping

Accounting is not bookkeeping. Bookkeeping concentrates on recording the organization's financial activities, whatever the business in which they are engaged. Maybe that is retail sales, home construction or manufacturing. No matter what business activity is taking place, someone must keep track of the transactions; selling, buying, repairing equipment, everything of significance. And in fact, even individuals must learn about accounting and must do certain bookkeeping tasks for their own personal finances, like balancing their checkbook and establishing personal budgets.

If the business is engaged in retail sales, bookkeepers record every sale, every purchase of inventory and every employee's pay. That is bookkeeping.

Accountants take this information and analyze, summarize and report the results. Remember, the product of accounting is information. This information is vital to management for their operating and investment decisions. Management must know how much money the business has, how much inventory it holds, how many employees are retained and how much they are being paid.

The viewpoint of a bookkeeper is the details. The viewpoint of an accountant is much broader and at a higher level. The accountant must be able to advise management on many decisions; how many more employees can be hired, what taxes are due and how to minimize them, analyzing investment decisions, and so forth.

Let's look at an example. Riverside Machine Company is a small manufacturer of components for the automobile industry. Their clients include almost all of the automobile manufacturers, and they are very busy when the industry is thriving.

The owners of Riverside are concerned about reducing manufacturing costs for a certain type of part that requires a lot of machining on several different types of machines. The engineers have determined that they can increase the rate of production by installing robots to load and unload the machines and transfer parts between them. The company has several robotic systems in operation now and is confident of their ability to incorporate these new robots. Currently, there is a serious backlog of work for these machines and improving the workflow would allow faster delivery with less overtime and not needing to work weekends to maintain production.

The engineers have determined all the necessary information related to this investment in terms of robot costs, tools needed by the robots, increases in production rate and effect on delivery time. They then sit down with the accounting experts to compute the improvements in cost, reductions in labor costs, shortening of delivery time and so forth. The accountant then uses all of this information to compute the effects on the firm's financial performance and profitability.

In most companies, the accountants compute a value for "Internal Rate of Return" for decisions by management. This rate of return serves as a threshold for new projects. It becomes one of the considerations used by management to decide whether or not to make the investment, in this case, in the new robots. Other considerations of course include delivery improvements, customer satisfaction, product quality and several others. That is a proper role for the accountant working with the engineers.

In addition to being a source of reliable financial information on these kinds of decisions, the accounting department also acts as what can be described as a "Scorekeeper", by monitoring costs and revenues, leading to profitability for the firm. This information is reported to management on a regular basis to help guide ongoing management decisions. The accountants cannot do much at all to influence the profitability of the firm directly, but their role is to report findings to management for them to make decisions.

The accounting function also leads the efforts at budgeting and budget reporting. These are more examples of the accounting product of information. These reports are available in varying levels of detail for publically owned companies and non-profit organizations. Privately owned companies are not required to publish these reports, except for those required by the government, regulatory and taxing authorities.

In their role as providers of information, they are often called upon for informed recommendations to help management decision making.

# Chapter 2 - Understanding the Vocabulary

Every special area of interest has its own vocabulary, and accounting is the same. Many of the words used will be familiar to the reader but may have certain shades of meaning that are important. We need to understand this vocabulary. Here are some key definitions that are important to the accounting function.

**Asset:** an asset is anything the organization owns that helps it accomplish its mission. For a fast food restaurant, the grill or stove in the kitchen area is an asset. For a retail store, the inventory in the back room is an asset, along with display cases and shelves.

**Liability:** a liability is anything the organization owes to someone else. Unpaid wages to employees is a liability, taxes owed to the local government is a liability, unpaid insurance premiums for employee healthcare policies is a liability, bills for inventory that have not been paid is a liability.

**Equity:** equity is a measure of the claim of someone on the assets of the organization, such as liabilities (claims by the person or entity to whom the liability is owed, such as loans from a bank) and the investment by the owners of the organization.

**Income:** money flowing into the organization from its operations in whatever the line of business might be, for example, sales in a fast food restaurant, or rent collected on property the business owns.

**Expense:** this is the amount of money the organization needs to spend in order to carry out its operations. This represents payments to asset and service providers. For example, payments to a supplier of inventory items for a retail store.

**Distributions**: outflows of money to owners or stockholders, or bonuses to employees at the end of the year, for example.

**Cash Flow:** the term cash flow represents the money flowing through the operation, essentially income minus expenses. You can imagine a stream of money flowing into the organization with small streams going out as distributaries to pay for liabilities. The flow that is moving through this stream is the cash flow. How much is left at the end of the process is the profit for the firm.

**Overhead:** this is a group of costs not directly associated with the major function of the organization but necessary in order to make the organization accomplish its goals. For example, in a hospital, the janitorial staff that cleans and sanitizes the buildings, rooms and equipment are not directly associated with the hospital's patients, but they are absolutely essential. The labor and other costs like cleaning and sanitizing supplies are part of the organization's overhead. All the other myriad of costs like electricity, lighting, lawn maintenance, and even sweeping the parking lot are essential but not directly tied to the patients and their care. The accounting office is considered overhead for any organization not involved in the Public Accounting business.

**GAAP:** This is the term used to describe the Generally Accepted Accounting Principles. This is a set of 'rules' for the accounting profession, which must be followed to assure an accurate description of the financial activities of the organization. GAAP applies to all organizations that function in commerce, public service, and all other sectors of the general economy. Following these GAAP rules assures the public, the stockholders, the donors to non-profit organizations, the owners, employees and the taxing and regulatory authorities that the accounting for the organization is done in accordance with the proper methods and systems.

Each country establishes its own accounting standards but there exists an International Accounting Standards Board responsible for establishing and accrediting accounting standards for all nations who subscribe. Similarly, many countries establish similar Boards, to promulgate and enforce standards through certification and audit systems. These are in the form of standards, conventions and rules. Companies are not necessarily required to follow them but any publicly traded company must conform to the established Accounting Practices.

# Chapter 3 – Accounting Reports: The Income Statement

Remember that the product of accounting is information. The three most common forms for that information are the "Income Statement", the "Balance Sheet", and the "Cash Flow Statement." Every organization uses some form of these three documents and usually all three. We will explore the Balance Sheet in Chapter 4 and the Cash Flow Statement in Chapter 5.

The Income Statement or Profit and Loss Statement (or P&L statement) can be imagined as a video tape of the organization over some period of time, like a month, six months or a year. This statement tells management how the firm is doing from the standpoint of "Are we making money or not?" Of course, this is a very fundamental question, since after a number of periods of losses, the firm will no longer be viable and will go out of business.

The most important use of the Income Statement is to compare it with prior periods and with the period budget. If management has determined that the firm must meet certain performance levels, they need the answer to the question above; "How are we doing compared with our goals and budget?" Each organization has an established and agreed upon budget. The budget contains allocations of resources for all of the activities of the organization, from sales, purchases of materials for sale or production, employee salaries and benefits and even overhead items like electricity and water.

These budgets are set up, usually each year, to guide the managers and supervisors in what decisions can be made to commit resources like money and labour, and for what purposes. Based on this budget, which has been agreed upon by management, it acts as a steering mechanism for the firm's operations. The periodic P&L reports represent the Accounting function's role in keeping score. Here is an example of a P&L Statement or an Income Statement. We will look at each of these entries to see what they represent, based on The Martin Company.

# THE MARTIN COMPANY, INC.

## INCOME STATEMENT

## (FIRST HALF, 2014)

## JANUARY 1, 2014 THROUGH JUNE 30, 2014

## (all amounts in thousands of dollars)

**Sales, Gross**: $116,410

Less: Returns and Allowances: $3,075

**Net Sales**: $113,335

Less Cost of Goods Sold: $78,683

Less Current Depreciation Charges: $1,450

**Gross Profit:** $33,202

**Operating Expenses**

Selling and Promotion: $18,005

General and Administration: $8,910

**Total Operating Expenses**: $26,915

**Operating Profit:** $6,287

(Gross Profit minus Operating Expense)

**Other Income and Expense**

Interest and Dividend Income: $363

less: Interest Expense: $917

Net Interest Expense: $554

**Profit Before Taxes:** $5,733

Taxes on Income at 35%: $2,007

**Net Profit**: $3,726

This P&L or Income Statement is for the Martin Company. The Martin Company manufacturers small household appliances, which are sold through distributors under Martin's label and major discount and department stores under their labels. Manufacturing operations are located in a small town in the Midwest. The key technologies employed by the firm include manufacturing of fractional horsepower motors, injection molding of plastic parts and machining of miscellaneous small metal parts such as shafts, armatures and gears as well as assembly of the products, packaging and shipping them to customers.

As it says at the top, this report covers the first half of the year. For this company, their budget year is a calendar year. Some organizations may use other budget years. Government organizations often use October 1 through September 30 as a budget year. A mid-year report is very valuable to management, to keep track of performance, especially in complex organizations.

Total Sales; The first line entered is the total sales for that period. This is the value of products shipped to customers. In some cases, there may be returns from customers for any number of reasons; wrong color, wrong address, quality issues, and so forth. This is recorded as Returns and Allowances and is subtracted from Gross Sales resulting in Net Sales.

Cost of Goods Sold; The line labeled Cost of Goods Sold represents the cost that Martin incurred in producing the products shipped during that period. That will include the materials and components purchased, the labor used to produce these products and may include machine time if that is the procedure for Martin Company.

Depreciation; Martin Company must also account for the wear and tear on their productive assets ranging from big, expensive plastic injection molding machines to company vehicles. This is a real cost that must be accounted for but is not a cash expense. It is determined by the accounting office and along with the Cost of Goods Sold, reduces the net sales to give the amount of Gross Profit. This loss of value of assets is called depreciation and is subtracted from sales, even though it is not a cash expense. Depreciation will be covered in a later section.

Operating Expenses; However, this is not the complete picture of costs incurred. The items labeled Operating Expenses include the salaries of the supervisors, managers, sales representatives, shipping operators, energy costs like electric power and gas, office expenses for papers, copiers, and the myriad of other costs necessary to produce the products that generate sales income. In some companies, this lump of costs may be referred to as "Overhead." Overhead is a necessary expense and must be included in the budget and in P&L statement. Managers and supervisors work hard to keep Overhead costs to a minimum. Overhead also includes taxes paid on the real estate and other ad valorum taxes. These amounts are shown as Selling and Promotion as well as General and Administrative or G&A. G&A usually includes the Overhead costs.

Operating Profit; After accounting for the Operating Expenses, we are left with the Operating Profit. Operating Profit is the first measure of how effective Martin Company is in carrying out its main objective, making and selling products. Operating Profit is the Gross Profit minus the Operating Expenses.

Other Income and Expense; But, Martin Company must also take into account the other costs such as interest on loans they need to purchase equipment and materials. They may have other incidental income from sources like investments, rental property receipts and royalties. These are all included in the P&L statement but are not part of the major business, making and selling products.

Profit Before Taxes; When all of that is included, we see the Profit Before Taxes or PBT. That profit must be reduced by the taxes paid on the sales and other income, and we finally get to see the profits resulting from the major business of Martin. This is what managers call the "Bottom Line."

Managers and supervisors are vitally concerned with how the P&L Statement compares with the budget and how it is changing over time. Are we earning more profit this year than we did in the same period last year and in prior years? Continual growth in profit makes it possible of Martin to stay in business, producing products, serving customers and employing people. It is also essential to being able to expand the business, adding more products and investing in advanced technologies that customers demand.

# Continue Reading!

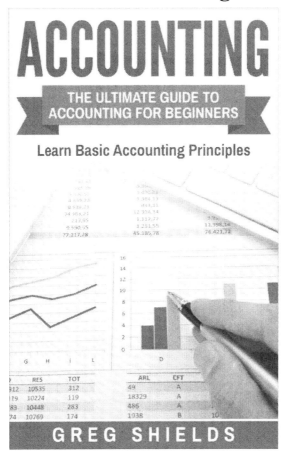

## Check out this book!

Made in the USA
Lexington, KY
29 January 2018